Enterta

Kevin Comber

Contents

Introduction 3

Magician: Ray Crowe 4

   The 'Magical Knot' trick 8

Storyteller: Dorinda Hafner 10

Clown: 'Fritz Sandwich' 17

Index 25

Glossary 25

Introduction

Entertainers are people who amuse us. They might be paid entertainers or friends who are clever and can make us laugh.

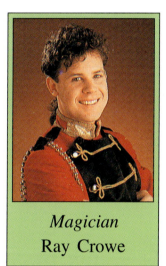

Magician
Ray Crowe

Storyteller
Dorinda Hafner

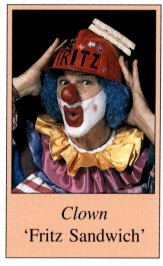

Clown
'Fritz Sandwich'

This book is based on interviews with three people who are paid entertainers. It describes how each person became an entertainer, and what they enjoy about their jobs. Each entertainer also gives hints or trade secrets about his or her work.

Magician: Ray Crowe

Ray Crowe is a magician. He can make people see things that really they do not. This is the art of illusion.

"When I was six years old I received a magic kit for Christmas and I was interested from then on."

Ray, aged 6, with magic kit

He gradually bought or borrowed lots of books about magic. When Ray was a teenager, a magician living in his street taught him some 'sleight of hand' tricks.

"This means I didn't hide these tricks behind boxes or veils, but learned to be quick and nimble with my hands and fingers."

His first trick was to make a coin disappear and then pull it out from behind someone's ear.

"A lot of the magic I am doing now, I have been doing since I was twelve years old and I've just been perfecting it. When I am working on a new routine, it can take up to a month or more of work before I am ready to let anyone see it."

Ray gave us a wonderful summary of the basic things that magicians do. They seem to make things:

- change colour;

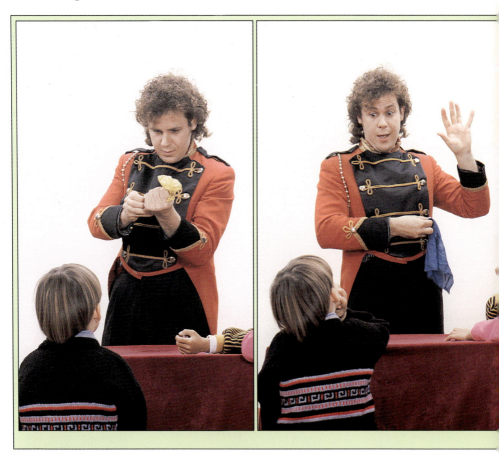

- move from one place to another;
- change weight so that they float;
- change shape;

- vanish or appear.

Ray does not talk on stage.

"I have studied mime . . . so I can work with anyone, anywhere and use mime techniques to entertain and communicate . . . You get to play with people, and that's nice."

"Probably the tricks that look the hardest are the easiest and the ones that look the easiest are the hardest!"

Sleight of hand tricks with cards or coins are actually very difficult to do smoothly. Tricks with boxes, for example, where the magician seems to cut through a person inside a box, are actually easy to perform.

The 'Magical Knot' trick

You show the audience a handkerchief. You place both ends of the handkerchief in one hand, then flick one end away. The audience discovers that there is now a knot in the handkerchief. How did it get there?

1. You need one large handkerchief.

2. Tie a knot in one end before you are in front of your audience.

3. Hold the knotted end between the thumb and forefinger of one hand. Close your hand to hide the knot.

4. Hold the other end between your first and second fingers.

5. As you flick the handkerchief away, let go of the knotted end only.

Storyteller: Dorinda Hafner

Dorinda Hafner is a storyteller as well as being an actor and musician and cook. She does a lot of work in schools telling stories about African culture. Storytelling has always been part of her life.

"Every single day from childhood until the age of eighteen I was told a story. Different members of the family built on stories I already knew. So I grew up hearing and telling stories. Other people told me stories about my life and about the area I lived in."

Dorinda tells fables which often contain animal characters. She uses stories to help children not to be frightened of something such as spiders or snakes. She also uses music and movement in her stories. She asks children to play characters. Dorinda laughs about the time she had all the staff and students at a school pretending to be calabash chickens.

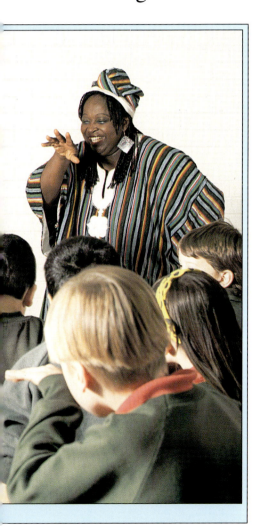

"One story that children particularly like is about a chicken. They get to play the chickens and I show them how chickens drink and they get to do a special chicken dance! They had their legs astride chairs with their bottoms stuck out ready to lay an egg!"

Dorinda also involves the audience in the action of the story by using the children as props, and other props, such as drums.

"Sometimes I take in fabrics, which the audience uses to swing and make the wind."

Dorinda explains that many African stories are long and children find it hard to sit and listen for a long time.

"I have to use a lot of energy to keep children interested. I also keep their interest by including a surprise ending, where the story continues and involves the children further."

A 'Donno'
— Ashanti talking-drum

She revealed other secrets on how to get the audience's attention.

"*I start off by getting the audience to use their energy. I might get them doing tribal calls and really using their voices like when they cheer for their teams! Then I often have them pretend that they are chewing gum!*

"I also use a lot of movement and music and change my voice to regain or hold attention. If a story goes wrong I stop and ask the children to help. I might forget a line and I will ask the children to remind me."

Dorinda recalls how she began storytelling in Australia.

"I worked on the television telling my stories . . . I also started a program called 'Africa in Schools' where I visit schools and explain African culture and let children experience it through music, storytelling, artefacts, drama, movement, cooking and talking with me."

Storytelling is an enjoyable and important part of Dorinda's life.

"I love watching the children's faces! Storytelling has helped me learn patience. It has helped me speak more clearly. It has helped me to learn to say some important words more loudly or slowly so that people know this bit is special. It has taught me to share. I also know I have the power to help people to change their thinking. I can help children to like people of other races and cultures by becoming a friend."

Dorinda believes we need to understand how important storytelling skills are. Storytellers often gain confidence to speak up in almost any situation in their lives, not only when they are telling stories.

"Everyone should be a storyteller. You can start by telling about your day, your favourite shows on television, your friends. Just start with one thing and build your story from there. Part of the excitement of life for me is to constantly learn new things. I observe people and life. I always find something different. I don't think I'll ever finish learning!"

If you are thinking of being a storyteller you need:

- to tell stories about your own life;
- to enjoy telling stories;
- to change your voice to hold people's attention;
- to use a lot of energy to keep the audience interested;
- to involve the audience;
- to be ready to learn new things.

Clown: 'Fritz Sandwich'

'Fritz Sandwich' is a clown. His main job is to make people smile, laugh and feel happy.

Fritz ('Peter' is his real name) became a clown while delivering singing telegrams. His boss dared him to do a clown's job for a children's party! Peter had no idea that he would become a clown.

"It is my whole working life. It is what I do."

Fritz has to practise a lot. His room has a lot of mirrors on the cupboard to help him see how he looks while he is practising his performance.

"I have a book and when I think of an idea for my act I write it down in the book."

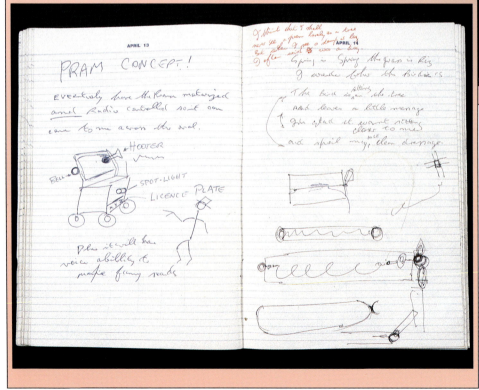

The first trick Fritz ever performed was a success.

"It was with a bowl of eggs. The top one was raw. I cracked it into a glass and drank it! All the other eggs were hard-boiled. Then I started to juggle the other eggs over the heads of the audience. The eggs dropped to the ground because I could not juggle. Everyone cried, 'Look out!' but were relieved to find that the eggs were hard-boiled and did not splatter."

Fritz' costumes change from year to year but he always uses the same make-up. He is always 'Fritz Sandwich'.

"I wear make-up over half of my face. I always wear a wig and a big, false red nose. I wear a hat sometimes. I wear ordinary-sized shoes but painted up so that they look a bit different."

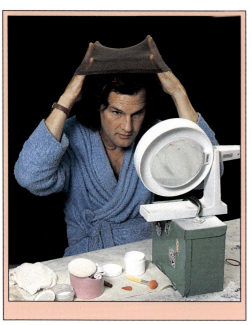 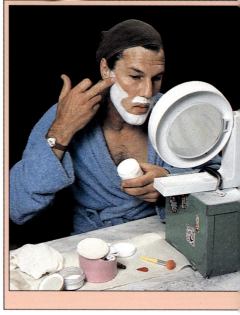

He also uses props in his routines.

"I use just about anything as props, making sure to use them for a funny purpose, such as putting saucepans on the head as hats, using an upside-down chair as a gymnasium, using egg beaters as propellers. The possibilities are endless!"

Fritz remembers that when he started he had no idea of how to keep rowdy people under control.

"If people get too excited it's hard to keep performing. Now, if all the children are over-excited or jumping up and down, I'll play 'Simon Says' with them and jump up and down too and help them to settle down."

 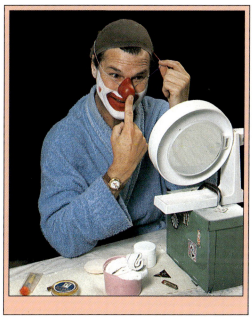

During a performance, Fritz might do what he calls 'laughs'. He explains what this means.

"Clown gags. You know . . . stinging myself with a balloon, bopping myself on the head with a soft hammer or dusting children off with a feather duster.

"I meet you and perhaps discover something imaginary on your shoulder. Even though I do this with one person, others around join in and laugh too. 'Shoes' is a good one: I like to try and swap shoes with children! The false handshake is a funny one. If kids give their right hand I give my left and vice versa. Sometimes a child will be quick enough to grab my hand and then I pretend there is glue on it and won't let the child's hand go easily!"

Fritz does lots of other things as part of his flexible routine, including bubble-blowing sessions where the audience joins in.

"I blow high and low bubbles so different aged kids can all be part of it. Clowning is not only making people laugh, but also helping them to have a good time. For instance, I also do magic tricks and make up stories as I go, to suit the audience."

His audiences like the parts of his routine where he appears to be hurt. He isn't really hurt, it only looks as if he is!

Fritz explains why he does not do slapstick 'pie in the face' routines.

"I can't do it, because I often can't go home and have a shower because I have another 'gig' to go to."

Fritz sums up his job as a clown.

"The best part of it is when children come up after the show and let you know they liked you. The worst thing about being a clown is the make-up! I'd rather grow a beard, but I can't because I need to put my clown make-up on. The make-up is very hard on the skin."

Fritz does not think everybody can be a clown.

"If you are thinking of it, you need:
- to want to make people laugh;
- to be happy to be looked at by groups of people;
- to start getting involved in acting;
- to take part in school plays;
- to learn to juggle."